Algebra

Desert Patterns

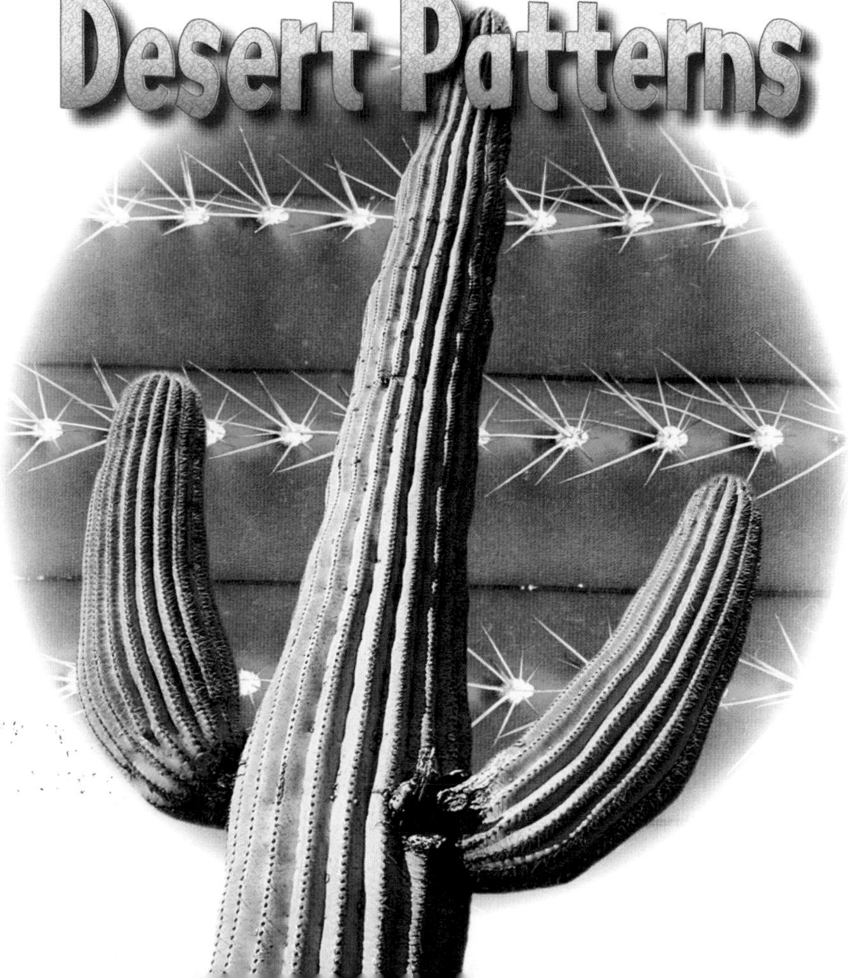

In this desert, what patterns can you see?

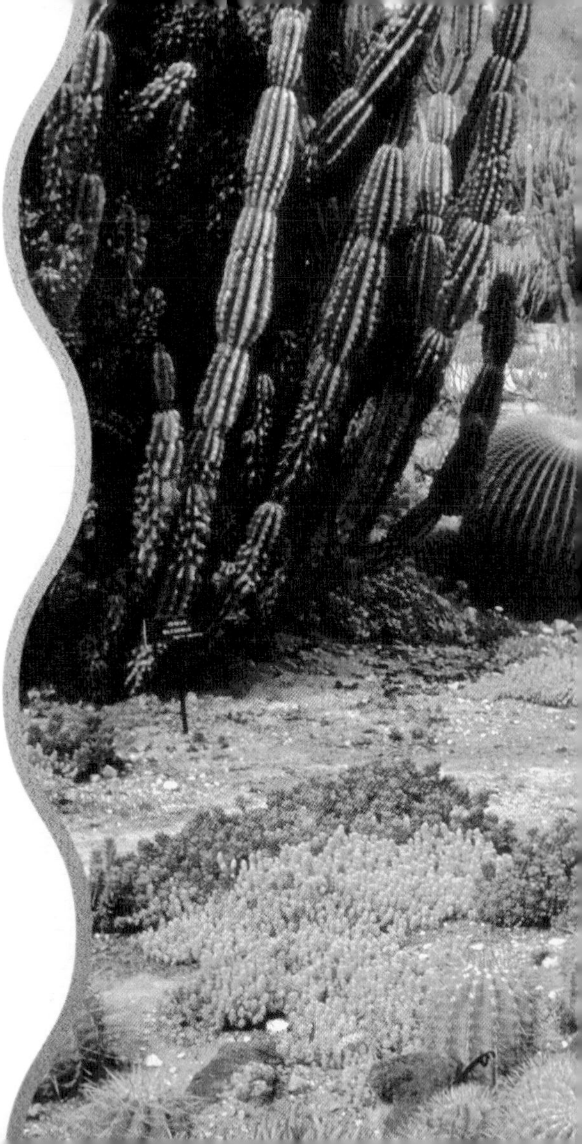

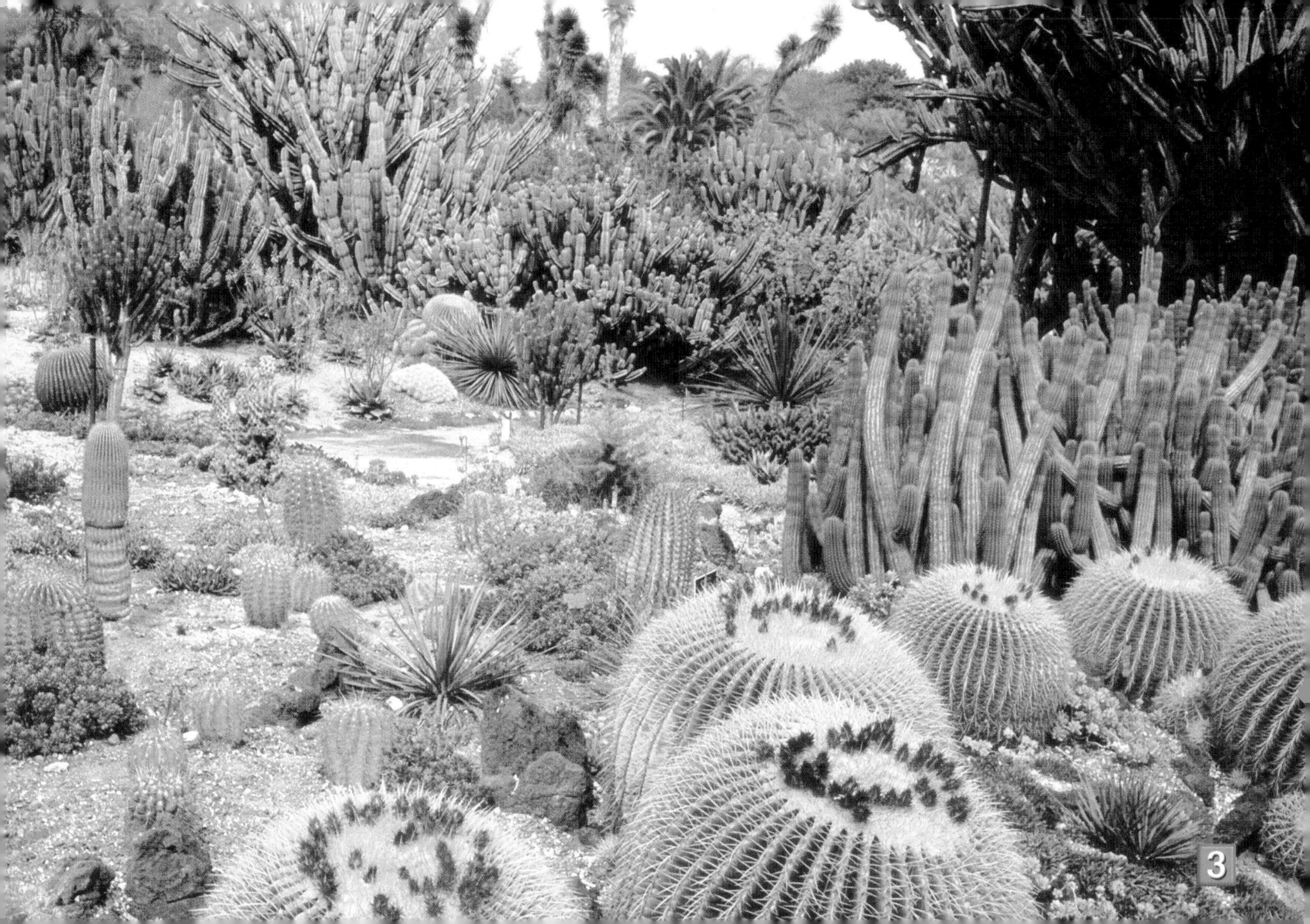
3

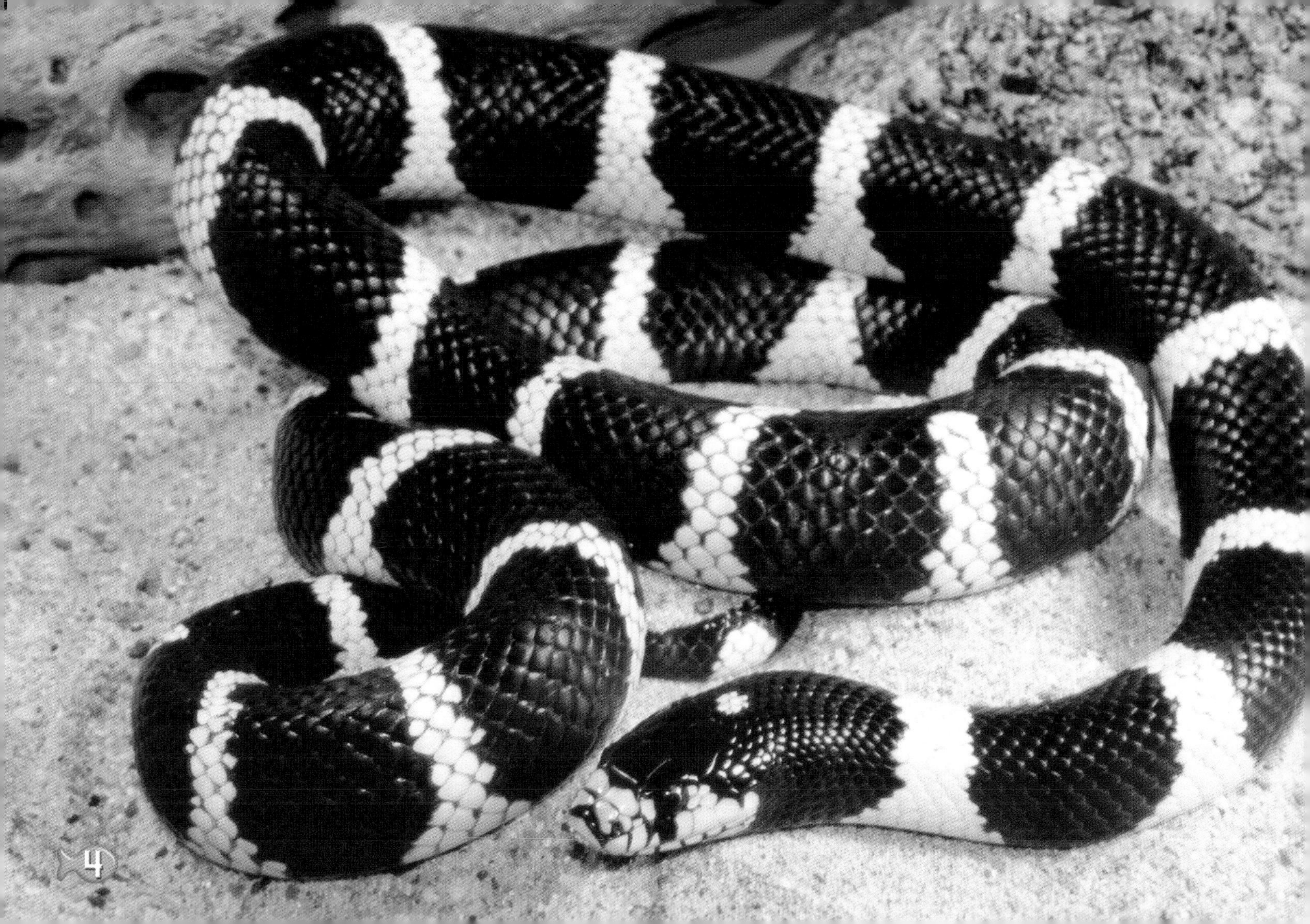

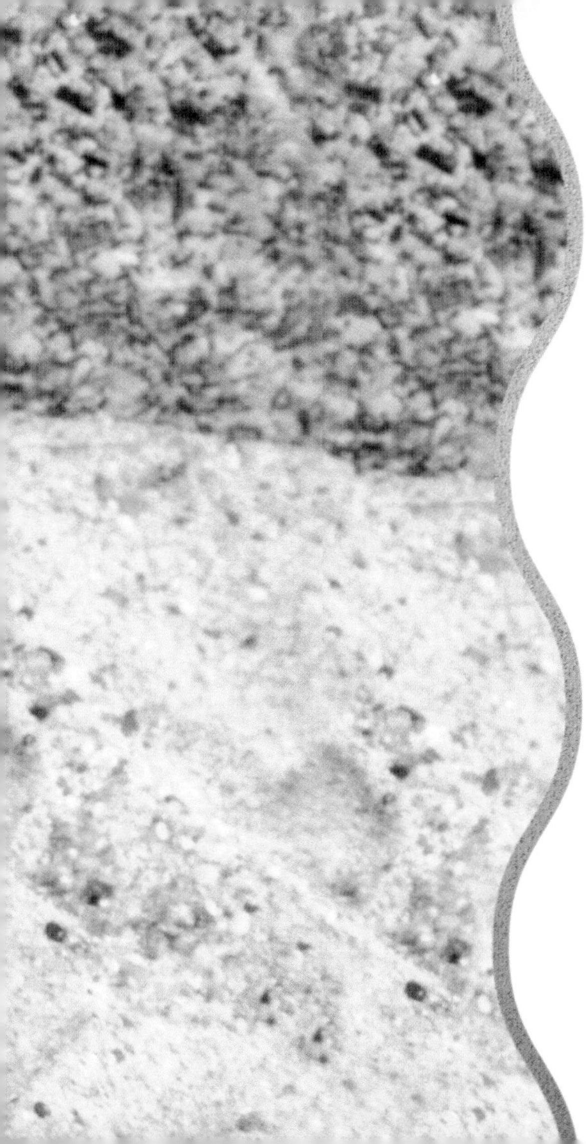

In this desert, what patterns can you see?

In this desert, what patterns can you see?

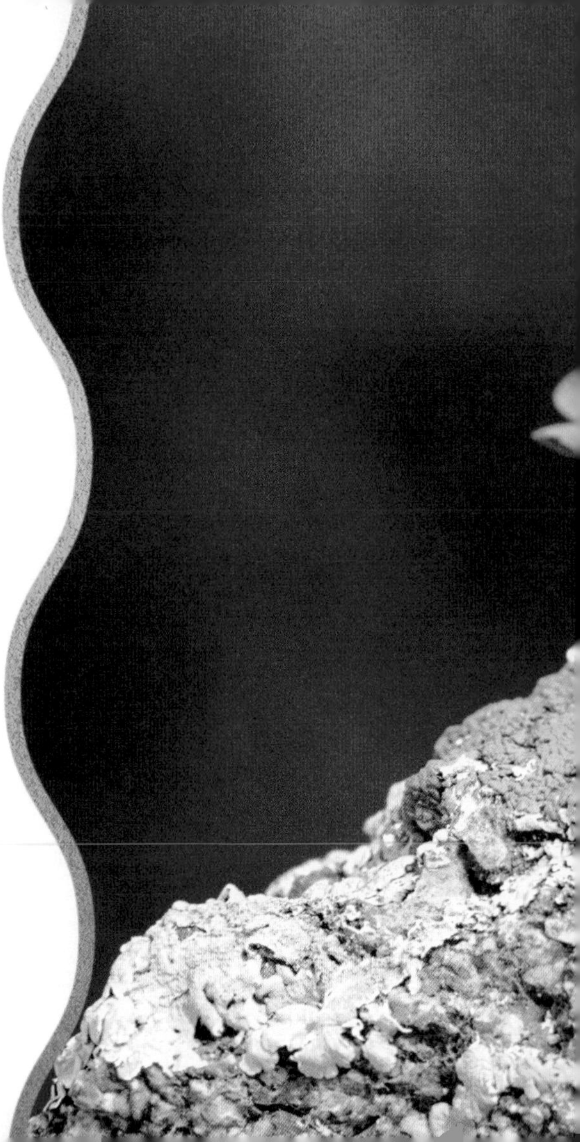

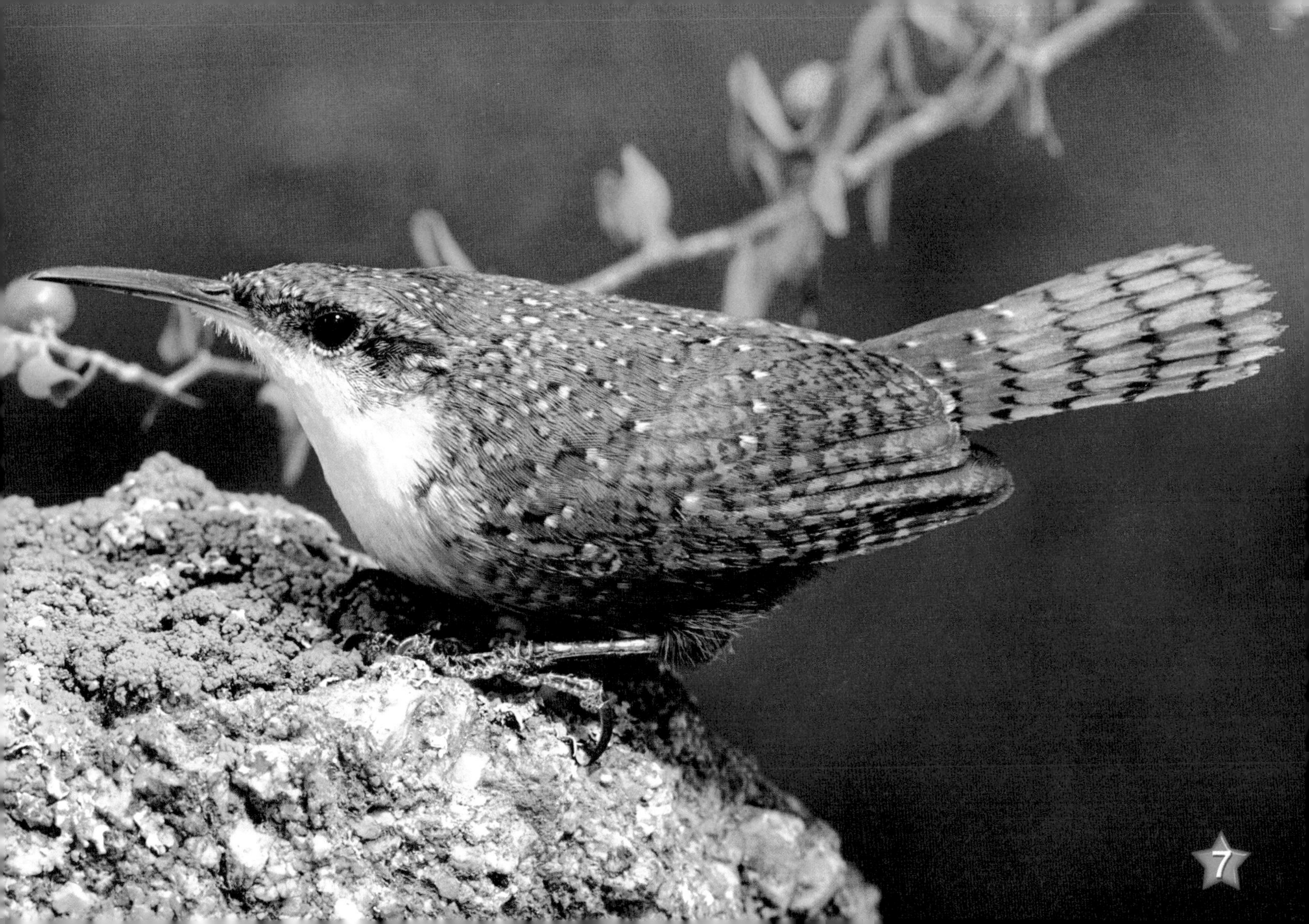

In this desert, what patterns can you see?

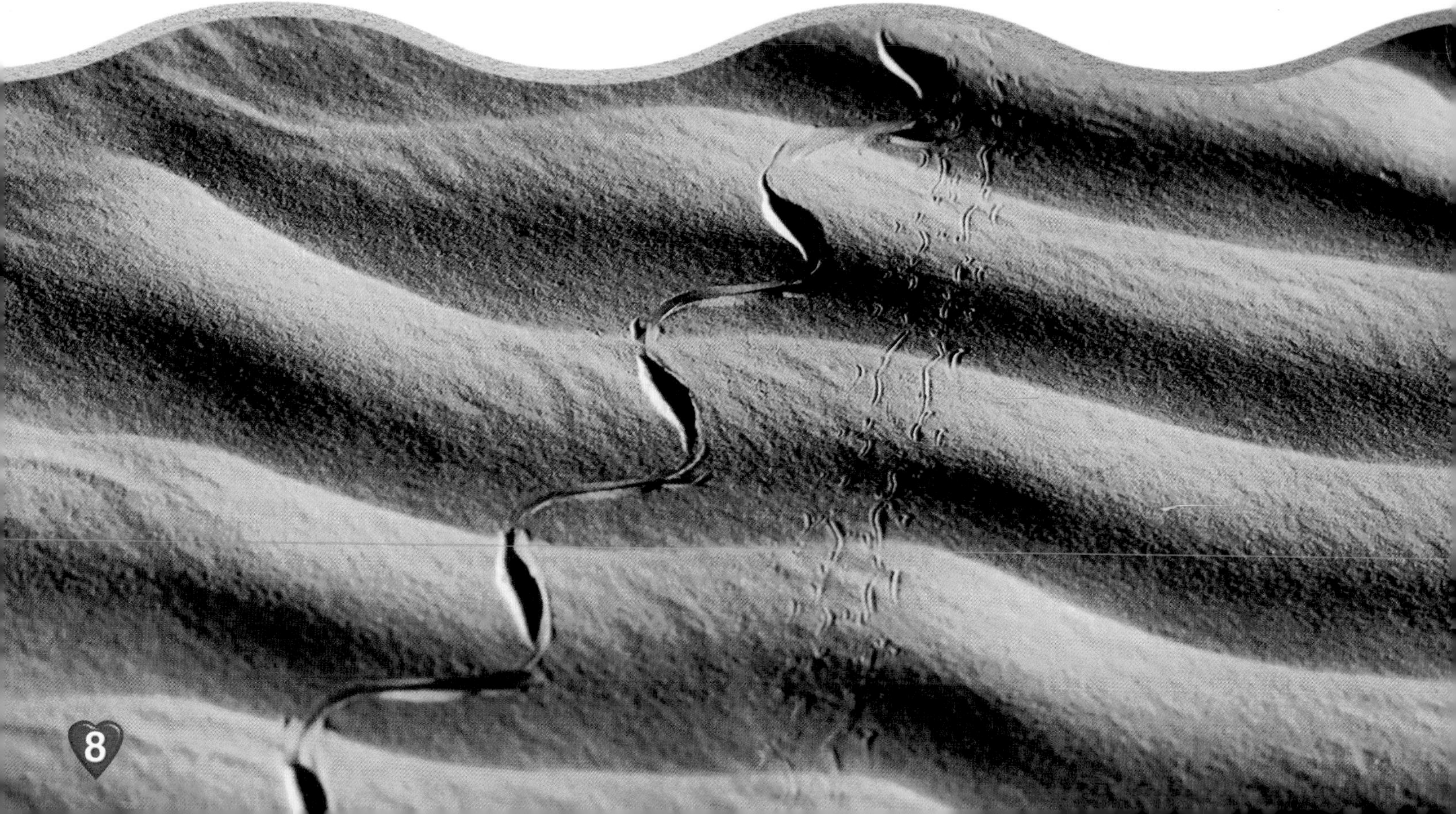